COCO CH

A Life from Beginning to End

Copyright © 2020 by Hourly History.

Table of Contents

Introduction

An Orphaned Girl

Coco Takes on Paris

The House of Chanel

Chanel No. 5

Another Failed Romance

The Little Black Dress

The Duke of Westminster

The Crash of 1929

Chanel during World War II: The Nazi Spy

Exile and Return

Conclusion

Introduction

Gabrielle "Coco" Chanel was born in France in 1883, at a time when the world was changing. She grew up in poverty and was sent to an orphanage at the age of 11. Education for poor girls was not encouraged, and the orphanage prepared girls for life by teaching them how to cook and sew. Sewing, and later designing, became Coco's lifeline. Her passion for fashion consumed her entire life. While still in her early twenties, she opened her first dress shop in Paris with the help of her lover.

Coco's designs were new and radical, and women loved them. She dispensed with the bustles and fuss of the Victorian and Edwardian eras and gave women simple designs made out of wearable material, such as jersey. Within a few years, she had three shops. Before she died, there would be Chanel stores throughout the world. Society women and even royalty flocked to her shops. Never quite one of them, always on the periphery of the elite, Coco straddled the life of a seamstress and friend of the world's elite. It was a delicate balancing act.

Coco's work gave her independence—something she craved. She took on many lovers, all of them members of the upper class and most of them married. Her reputation frequently suffered as a result, but she didn't care. None of these relationships lasted, however. Coco was frequently lonely, but unwilling to give up her independence or her work, for which she was becoming famous and rich. Although her distinct fashion was sought after, it was the creation of her signature perfume, Chanel No. 5, that made her name a household word. It was the world's most expensive scent and would ultimately make her a fortune.

Always remembering the bleak years at the orphanage, Coco Chanel surrounded herself with beauty and style. Every one of her homes was a masterpiece. Still, she spent much of her time living at the Hotel Ritz; she was unable to settle down and relax into domesticity.

Coco was forced to close her shops when the Germans invaded Paris during World War II. Her affair, and suspected collaboration, with a German officer came close to costing her everything. After the war, she was forced to flee to Switzerland without reopening the House of Chanel. At the age of 70, during the 1950s, she went back to work, but her collaboration with the Germans was not forgotten. Paris did not embrace her new designs. In addition, fashion had changed. Instead of Coco Chanel, it was Mary Quant who ruled the fashion world.

Coco continued working until her death in 1971. The sale of her perfume had made her a billionaire. Hated or loved, Coco Chanel was a legend in her own lifetime.

Chapter One

An Orphaned Girl

"My earliest childhood makes me shudder. No childhood was less gentle."

—Coco Chanel

The woman who would become a fashion icon for generations of women did not have a promising start in life. Gabrielle Bonheur "Coco" Chanel was born the second of five children to Albert Chanel and Jeanne Devolle on August 19, 1883. Her young parents were not married, and Albert refused even to acknowledge his two daughters. Albert was an itinerant salesman, taking his wagonload of wares from village to village without any intentions of settling down. Jeanne's family, from the village of Courpiere, were poor, but yearning for upward mobility. A daughter with two illegitimate children would be a stumbling block to that dream. It was a social embarrassment.

The entire Devolle family pleaded with Albert to marry Jeanne. He ignored them and simply kept on the move with his wagon filled with merchandise, returning to Courpiere on rare occasions and without supporting Jeanne or the children. Jeanne was forced to work as a domestic while her family took care of her children. For Albert, there were other women.

Sometimes, Jeanne and the children would accompany Albert. At other times, the children were parceled out to relatives who had no inclination to care for a bunch of unruly youngsters. Coco, especially rebellious, was stigmatized as the bad child.

Jeanne's uncle finally promised the couple a place to stay and some money if Albert would marry Jeanne. With tremendous reluctance, and after Jeanne's family paid him, he finally agreed. Still, he spent most of his time on the road, seeing little of his growing family. The children stayed with whatever family member would tolerate them for a short time.

This unstable existence lasted until Coco was 11 years old when, weakened by fever, Jeanne Chanel, died. Albert did not even pretend to care for his children and simply disappeared forever. Coco never saw her father again. She and her two sisters were sent to the convent at Aubazine, which took in charity cases. The convent was located far out of town and surrounded by a high wall. It was a virtual prison and would be Coco's home for the next six years.

While the girls were provided with a rudiment of writing and arithmetic, a real education was seen as a waste of time. These girls were poor; their best hope would be to marry some farmer and cook and clean. The less fortunate would enter servitude, which also involved cooking and cleaning. No learning was needed for such a miserable future. The orphanage did, however, emphasize sewing, a skill that would be useful to a poor woman after leaving the orphanage.

Later in life, when Coco Chanel became a member of the international elite set, she rarely wrote letters. Her spelling and grammar were embarrassing to her. She never did forget her loveless and neglectful upbringing. "Love is a luxury, and childhood is a sin." It was a luxury for which Coco would search in vain most of her life.

Following her six years of confinement, Coco finally tasted freedom. She moved to nearby Moulins in central France. It was a small town, but following Aubazine, it must have seemed exciting to a young girl out on her own. Her grandparents lived nearby, but Coco was not interested in developing a relationship. The bitterness she harbored toward her indifferent relatives would remain with her for the rest of her days.

She did, however, make her first friend, who also happened to be her aunt. Although Adrienne Chanel was her aunt, she was only two years older than Coco. Both girls found jobs as seamstresses at a draper's shop. There was an exclusive military regiment stationed in Moulins, so there was almost unlimited alteration work to be done for the soldiers, although the pay was pitiful. Coco could barely afford a small room in one of the less desirable parts of town.

Still, the town had much to offer two young girls. Surrounded by so many officers, they were rarely without admirers. They were soon escorted to the local café-concerts, the center of the town's social life. When a singer (usually female) sang her repertoire of songs, she was surrounded by a circle of local girls striking suggestive poses during the performance. These girls were known as poseuses, and they filled in for the songbird when she took a break. These cafés were the forerunners of what would develop into the famous cabarets in Paris.

Coco and Adrienne both became poseuses. Coco could not sing, nor was she particularly attractive, but she had personality and charm, and it didn't take her long to develop her own coterie of admirers. The two Chanel girls quickly became favorites with the officers.

One officer in particular who noticed Coco was Étienne Balsan, the son of a wealthy textile merchant. It is unknown whether Étienne was Coco's first lover, but the two soon began an affair. However, in the game of romance, Adrienne initially won the sweepstakes. She became the companion of a wealthy baron and spent the remainder of her life in luxury. Coco moved in with the somewhat less illustrious Étienne. Nevertheless, life at his château Royallieu was hardly shabby. Living well out of wedlock was a more desirable idea than living in poverty. As a wealthy man, Étienne had the luxury of not caring about his reputation. Coco was not as fortunate. In the 1906 census, she was listed as a "kept woman," or mistress.

Going from being the daughter of an itinerant salesman to orphan to becoming the mistress of a wealthy upper-class lover had to be a shock to Coco's system. At the château, she was surrounded by every imaginable luxury. Servants did her bidding. She rode horses and read romances. All it cost her was her reputation and respectability.

Coco enjoyed the good life, but her future was on her mind. She knew that mistresses were invariably discarded at some point. Then what would happen to her? Her imagination was stirred during a visit to a Parisian department store. Instead of dresses, she bought a number of hats. At the time, ladies' hats were huge and filled with all types of adornments. At the château, Coco reworked the hats to make them plainer—they became simple and elegant. The women who saw them loved them. The era of Victorian and Edwardian fussiness was gone. It was a new century, with new ideas. Women were no longer walking around wearing an elaborate flower garden on top of their heads. Coco was well in-tune with the times.

Coco begged Étienne to help her open a millinery shop. He refused. No matter—there were other men in her life. By this time, Coco had entered into a relationship with one of Étienne's friends, the British shipping merchant and polo player Arthur Capel. Capel was supportive of Coco's ideas and set her up in his brother's Paris apartment and provided her with funds to open her first shop.

Coco Chanel's career as a milliner was about to take off.

Chapter Two

Coco Takes on Paris

"My work came about as a reaction to my times."

—Coco Chanel

Coco left Étienne to become Arthur Capel's mistress. Such sophisticated games were not particularly unusual in their social set. As a matter of fact, the three even remained friends. In 1910, Arthur helped Coco finance a small shop called at 21 rue Cambon in Paris, where she was soon employing three assistants. It was surrounded by other luxury shops and a prime shopping location. From the very beginning, Coco had unerring business acumen.

In 1913, Paris was changing. Foreign artists such as Pablo Picasso and Vaslav Nijinsky were turning accepted art on its head. Exercise for women, such as the long strolls taken by English women, were becoming fashionable. Changes in lifestyle meant that women were looking for a more comfortable way to dress. That year, Coco sold her first dress, a plain sheath with a simple collar.

The onset of World War I brought upheaval to Paris, however. Anyone who could leave the German-occupied city, did. The beau monde escaped to the resort town of Deauville, and Arthur and Coco were among those who sought safety down south. Life in Deauville revolved around the beach and its famed boardwalk. Coco immediately recognized the opportunity. Before Arthur enlisted in the army, he helped her finance a shop in the best part of town. Here, she designed simple skirts and redid men's shirts into a more feminine style. Sweaters were loose and draped. Instead of silks or other fashionable material that would get ruined in the sand, she opted for jersey. Not only was it more comfortable, but it was also an inexpensive material during wartime shortages.

Ladies eager for comfortable resort wear flocked to her new shop. Figuratively, if not literally, corsets and petticoats were tossed to the wind. Coco's designs concentrated on structure instead of embellishments as she was raising hemlines and loosening the waistline. Even the wealthy were eschewing the ostentation of pre-war dresses. When Baroness Diane de Rothschild became a customer, Coco's reputation was made. The war was actually working to her advantage. She and her three seamstresses were kept extremely busy. In 1915, she even opened a third shop in Biarritz.

Her use of jersey soon caught the attention of America's *Woman's Wear Daily*. For years to come, Coco Chanel would be associated with jersey, a material used for men's underwear but found to be too scratchy. By 1916, Coco was being mentioned in *Vogue*, "The liking for jersey has developed into a passion." When World War I came to an end, Coco Chanel stood as a revolutionary of women's fashion. According to *Harper's Bazaar,* "The woman who doesn't have at least one Chanel is hopelessly out of the running." The girl who had suffered for years in a charity orphanage was becoming world-renowned.

In 1916, Coco was able to repay her lover, Arthur Capel, his investment. Arthur supported her work while at the same time lamenting her newfound independence and fame. He would have preferred her to be less driven and more dependent on him. Coco made sure this did not happen. Before long, Arthur's attention was caught by Diana Wyndham, the aristocratic daughter of Lord Ribblesdale. Diana was the essence of uncomplicated femininity, which was an attraction after Coco's unbridled ambitions. The two women were polar opposites. Coco had no choice but to grudgingly accept her rival.

When he was with Coco, Arthur was by no means in control. If the couple was invited to parties with the elite set, it was invariably Coco who received all the attention. Many of her well-to-do clients had become her friends, and she was socializing with them as an equal. The former struggling seamstress was basking in her new glory.

By 1918, Coco was back in Paris, which was under German attack. Still, the social elite would not let war stand in the way of fashion. Coco's Paris salon was one of the first showrooms that paraded live models in front of potential buyers. During one occasion, a German bomb exploded and shattered all of the glass. The well-trained models continued their strut as if nothing had happened.

When the buyers, who were staying at the nearby Ritz, asked Coco what to wear during a potential evening raid, Coco immediately bought an array of men's silk pajamas and offered them to her female clients as a practical solution. Even during an enemy attack, the elite felt the need to be properly dressed, and Coco was happy to accommodate them.

At the same time, Arthur and Diana decided to get married. Coco was devasted. She had lost her love when she found her new independence. It was not an easy trade. She had been abandoned in childhood but had strived to overcome her humble beginnings. Now, the only man she had ever loved was making it clear that he still did not consider her good enough to marry. Arthur and Diana's wedding on August 3 caused her to have a minor breakdown. Arthur, who had truly cared for Coco, suffered similar emotional despair.

Coco obviously needed to move out of their shared Paris apartment. With many Parisians fleeing the city, she had no difficulty in finding a large and elegant apartment of her own at 6 quai Debilly. This would be the first apartment that Coco financed on her own. She also hired a couple to help her maintain her new living quarters.

At the age of 35, Coco began to question her attractiveness. There were, however, no lack of admirers. At the end of the year, she began affairs with an old, now married friend, Henri Bernstein, and Argentine millionaire Paul Eduardo Martínez de Hoz. She celebrated Armistice Day with Paul de Hoz. In the meantime, Arthur was demanding that his new wife dress herself in Chanel creations. He began to visit Coco at her new apartment. Sadly, Arthur died in an automobile accident in December 1919. Coco wrote, "His death was a terrible blow to me . . . I lost everything when I lost Capel."

Arthur clearly regretted giving up Coco. In his will, he bequeathed her 40,000 pounds.

Chapter Three

The House of Chanel

"Capel entrusted Gabrielle to me and a man like you is known as a shit."

—Misia Sert, to Igor Stravinsky regarding his affair with Coco Chanel

In early 1920, Coco was ready to open a new salon in Paris, although she kept the old one at 21 rue Cambon operational. Her new place was next door at 31 rue Cambon and was comprised of five floors. For the first time, she registered as "couturier" instead of "seamstress." She was successfully moving up the social ladder.

She also bought a new villa, Bel Respiro, for herself. It turned out that this was the same villa Arthur had bought for Diana a year earlier. Coco was perfectly aware of this, and Bel Respiro was to become her refuge and tribute to her memories of Arthur. In a strange way, she had found a way to live with her old lover again.

In an effort to pull her out of her state of near-madness and grief, her old friend Misia Sert persuaded Coco to accompany her and her new husband to Venice. Misia herself had been through several stormy affairs and understood Coco's pain. Coco agreed to the trip. While traveling through Padua, the group stopped at the Basilica of Saint Anthony. Perhaps some of the convent teachings were still with Coco. Praying to the saint, she found herself suddenly at peace. As she told Misia, "I took new heart and decided I wanted to live." She concluded that Arthur was on the other side, waiting for her. It was a comforting thought.

In Venice, Coco immersed herself in the great art of the past, as well as spending hours at street fairs. She met several famous artists, including the composer Igor Stravinsky. Although Coco would forever mourn the loss of Arthur Capel, once she returned to Paris, her old self emerged.

In the meantime, Stravinsky had become smitten with Coco. When he was back in Paris, he needed a house for his ill wife and four children. Kindly, Coco suggested he stay at Bel Respiro while she took a suite at the Hotel Ritz. Stravinsky was struggling financially and grateful for the offer. He and Coco began an affair. His music, a departure from the Romanticism to which audiences were accustomed, was not being well received. Under the sponsorship of Coco Chanel, he began the process of restaging his 1913 ballet, *The Rite of Spring*. Coco continued to sponsor Stravinsky for several years.

Her association with Stravinsky gave her an entrée into the top of artistic society. It was another social step up for the former orphan. Now, she was not only dressing the beau monde, but she was also influencing their artistic tastes. She had earned her own wealth and was determined to use it for whatever she saw fit. It brought her more of the independence she so desired.

On the day before New Year's Eve, Coco and Stravinsky threw an elaborate party for the Parisian artistic community at her offices on rue Cambon. The guests were a who's who of modern artists. This was a new and rarified world for Coco, and one she was anxious to become a part of.

When Stravinsky left with the Ballets Russe for Spain, he begged Coco to come. She was unwilling to commit herself, and Stravinsky was soon off on his own.

Chapter Four

Chanel No. 5

"The most costly perfume in the world."

—Coco Chanel

Coco wasn't on her own for long, and her next suitor would prove to be one of her most interesting. Grand Duke Dmitri Pavlovich was a cousin of the assassinated Tsar Nicholas II, and his life had been extremely privileged. In certain circles, he was considered the rightful tsar of Russia.

In 1916, Dmitri had been one of the conspirators in the killing of Grigori Rasputin, the mystic who had had a strong hold over the Tsarina Alexandra. Following the deaths of the royal family, Dmitri sought refuge first in England, then in Paris. He and Coco had met briefly at one of Arthur Capel's parties.

They renewed their acquaintance at a dinner party in 1921. Before long, they began seeing each other, and the gossips' tongues started to wag. Misia, who had turned quite spiteful, sent a telegram to Stravinsky in Spain. "Coco is a little shop girl who prefers Grand Dukes to artists." This ended whatever relationship she still had with Stravinsky. The composer was furious at having been tossed for a handsome royal such as Dmitri.

Coco was smitten. When Dmitri expressed a desire to see Monte Carlo, she bought a Rolls-Royce Silver Cloud for the trip. Secretly, the couple headed south to the Palace of Monte Carlo, one of the Mediterranean's most luxurious hotels. They spent their days lunching at the finest restaurants and their evenings at the casino. It was a rarified life that Dmitri was accustomed to, but Coco was not.

Their need to keep their relationship secret was due to the fact that Coco was paying for their holiday. Most of the Russian royals had lost all their wealth following the revolution, but Dmitri did not want to be seen as a "kept man." For Coco, paying for their trip was a way of being in control and utterly independent of any man. Coco was a modern woman, living life on her own terms.

The holiday did much to revive Coco's troubled spirits following Arthur's death and the drama with Stravinsky. The only serious mishap happened on their return drive to Paris. Inadvertently, Dmitri took a wrong turn, one that led right past the site of Arthur's accident and the cross erected by Coco. According to Dmitri's diary, she became devastated and depressed. Dmitri made a note of the road, which was straight without any obstacles. How had the accident happened? Arthur had clearly been torn between his wife, Diana, and his mistress, Coco. Without any clear answer, had he decided that the only solution was suicide? In Coco's mind, this must have been a real possibility and one that would haunt her for a long time. Upon their return to Paris, Dmitri and Coco parted amicably and returned to their normal lives.

In the 1920s, society ladies were still flocking to Coco's salon for a must-have Chanel creation. Her clothes remained distinctive. Fashion magazines such as *Vogue* wrote enthusiastically about Coco's unfailing, perfect taste.

She was especially lauded for ridding women of the dreaded corset. For women who weren't as slim as she, Coco did still sell corsets on the side. Her dresses were more tailored toward thin, androgynous bodies, such as herself. When it came to her designs, Coco was her own best advertisement.

The next important man in Coco's life was not to be a lover. Instead, Ernest Beaux was to create one of the world's most famous perfumes, Chanel No. 5. As renowned as her clothes became, Chanel would not be a brand without its trademark perfume. Like Coco herself, with her short hair, short skirts, and independent lifestyle, Chanel No. 5 would represent the modern, twentieth-century woman. The iconic scent would surpass even her designer clothes in fame.

The creation of this famous perfume is clouded in secrecy. It is unknown how the two met or how the scent was made. Ernest Beaux came from a French family dealing in perfumes in Russia, where he was celebrated for using unique ingredients. Like Dmitri, he was forced to flee Russia following the revolution. It is thought that Dmitri introduced him to Coco. Beaux was particularly known for using synthetic ingredients instead of heavy florals in his scents. According to Coco, "I wanted to give women a perfume, but an artificial perfume . . . I don't want rose or lily of the valley." She wanted something far more subtle. Coco had a hyperactive sense of smell and couldn't tolerate anyone who didn't "smell good."

Beaux had done experimentations with the organic compound known as aldehyde. This chemical was to revolutionize the world of perfumes. When Coco was told that some of the ingredients would be expensive, she said, "Add more. I would like to create the most costly perfume in the world." She wanted her perfume to be as exclusive as her clothes. Chanel chose the name Chanel No. 5 for her new fragrance for the simple reason that it was the fifth sample she had received from Beaux, and she was presenting her new dress collection in her salon on May 5.

Coco had Beaux make hundreds of sample bottles of Chanel No. 5 before she began selling the perfume in her store. Besides being a creative designer, she was proving herself to be a master at sales. While dining in restaurants, she would spray other customers who passed her table. In her salon, she had her assistants spray the air with the new scent and presented samples as gifts for her customers. People appreciated the wonderful smell. She created enough interest that when bottles began to appear in her stores, it appeared she was merely answering a general interest. It made her clientele feel important and appreciated.

Coco also worked hard at creating just the right bottle to suit the Chanel brand. In 1921, L'Eau de Chanel was on the market. Like all of Coco's creations, it stood out for its simplicity. The bottle itself has not changed in a hundred years. The intertwined letter C that appeared on the bottle became the logo for the entire Chanel enterprise.

Chapter Five

Another Failed Romance

"What remains clear is that with all my heart I give you my love, and all that follows doesn't matter."

—Pierre Reverdy, in a poem to Coco Chanel

With almost unlimited funds at her disposal, Coco moved to the Hôtel de Lauzan on Faubourg Saint-Honoré. It was a grand mansion with magnificent formal gardens. Coco took over the entire first floor. Eventually, she would take over the whole manor. She was completely overwhelmed with the rich grandeur of the building and set about decorating it to suit her particular tastes. Floor to ceiling mirrors covered several rooms. She furnished her new abode with mostly Louis XIV antiques with some added Chinese touches, such as large, colorful screens. She did her bedroom entirely in beige, a trademark Chanel color, with a fur throw for the bed. Space and luxury abounded in this palatial setting.

Her new home was run smoothly and effortlessly by a competent staff of servants. While Coco still ran her shops during the day, evenings were now devoted to almost frantic entertainment. A piano was installed, and her get-togethers were filled with the top artists of the day, including Stravinsky, who had returned from Spain. Jean Cocteau was a firm fixture at the party on Faubourg Saint-

Honoré. The music lasted well into the early hours. Coco even provided the painter Picasso with a room of his own, to be used whenever he didn't want to feel alone. They occasionally spent the night together, but neither sought anything more permanent.

Coco had been embroidering some of her creations since 1917. In 1921, Dmitri's sister, Maria Pavlovna, suggested that she do the embroidering for Coco. Like most Russian émigrés, Maria needed to find a way to make a living. She set up her own workshop and began working for the House of Chanel. She loved seeing her work displayed on Coco's clothes and worn by Coco's clientele. She was also fascinated by how Coco worked.

Coco never designed her dresses on paper. She would use a piece of material and drape it around a model—always someone tall and thin. A fitter would hand her pins. It was a very rigid process. No one spoke as Coco created her designs. If she felt it necessary to issue an order, it was obeyed immediately without question or contradiction. Coco was a general leading a fashion army into battle.

During her bi-annual showings, she always found a unifying theme. Her name was known by now for its unique designs, and her showings extremely popular. Buyers came from throughout Europe and America. Perhaps it was a bit of affectation that had Coco post a police guard in front of her salon during the showings. For the showing itself, the best and most coveted seats were on the top steps of the staircase paneled with mirrors leading down into the main showroom. The staircase still exists today. American buyers made up the largest portion of her sales. America, always less fussy and more casual than Europe, readily embraced her easy-to-wear style.

In addition to embroidering, Maria learned a lot about personal style from Coco. Like many refugees, Maria had paid scant attention to her looks. Coco found that abhorrent. Nothing mattered more to her than appearance. She taught Maria how to wear make-up and demanded that the girl cut her hair and lose weight. "If you wish to do business, the first thing to do is to look prosperous." Maria turned herself into a stylish version of Coco's wealthy clients.

By now, Coco was fully entrenched in the Parisian avant-garde artistic community. When Cocteau wrote a modern version of *Antigone*, he demanded that Coco design the costumes and Picasso create the scenery. The play became popular because people wanted to see creations by Coco Chanel and Picasso more than Cocteau's writing. Of the three artists, Coco received the most praise.

Coco's innovation didn't end with fashion. She and her artistic friends had discovered the village of Saint-Tropez in the French Riviera when it was still an unknown seaside hideaway. For the longest time, women had valued their creamy white skin and ensured that it remained so. White skin was a sign that one was rich enough not to have to work outdoors. Coco made sunbathing and having a tan fashionable. It seemed that whatever Coco did, others followed. Such was her impeccable sense of style.

By 1922, Coco was ready for another affair. Poet Pierre Reverdy was a member of the rebellious Montmartre clique. He was known for his distaste of the haut monde and the entire establishment. Of course, Coco had clawed her way up to become an admired part of the establishment. Still, she wasn't born into it. She was an outsider, a shop girl with enough talent to become wealthy. Reverdy was a part of the artistic group she enjoyed, and she found him intriguing. Their relationship was also an act of defiance against a society where she still wasn't quite at home.

Like many of Coco's lovers, Reverdy was married. Cocteau described him as "false, uncultured irascible." He ate and drank to excess. His raging temper caused him to lose many friends. Like Arthur, he wavered between wanting Coco and attempting to resist her. Where Reverdy was dark and pessimistic on sheer principle, Coco had unquenchable joie de vivre which he found impossible to resist.

As she had done with men before, Coco paid Reverdy's agent funds to be passed on to him, effectively financing his first major publication of poetry. All of this she did in secret, so as to enable him to maintain his pride. Paying her lovers was becoming a Coco Chanel habit.

Despite her best efforts, Reverdy left Paris with his wife in 1926. Coco had lost another lover. Once again, she was despondent. As Coco's business kept climbing toward the pinnacle of success, her romantic life kept collapsing. She seemed unable to stop herself from becoming entangled with inappropriate married men. At all times throughout her life, she remained reluctant to discuss her love life. Was she afraid of finding another true love, such as Arthur, only to lose him? With a complex person such as Coco Chanel, the actual facts are almost impossible to discern.

Chapter Six

The Little Black Dress

"Fashion, like landscape, is a state of mind, by which I mean my own."

—Coco Chanel

Coco's designs were quite revolutionary, and the line between art and craft could get blurred. She herself scorned the label of artist. She was a talented craftsman—anything else she considered pretentious.

To her, dresses weren't the equivalent of poetry or literature. As she stated, "fashion should express the place, the moment." It was intuitive awareness that made the moment clear to her. She was a woman of her time, which was rapidly changing. She paid attention to the world around her and incorporated her observations into her designs. In addition, she was shrewdly able to anticipate the next "moment," keeping her ahead of the competition. Art had longevity; fashion was immediate. At the same time, Coco was a firm advocate of following the current trend, whether or not it was attractive. Being in the here and now was important. As she stated, "No one is powerful enough to be more powerful than fashion."

Her own innate creativity allowed her to branch out from dressmaking. In 1924, she established a jewelry workshop under the supervision of Comte Étienne de

Beaumont. Beaumont wasn't a jeweler, but he had ordered several unique jewel designs for friends which Coco had admired.

While her clothing line was understated, Chanel's jewelry was bold and attention-getting. She especially loved strands of pearls, whether fake or real. Large, colorful stones were used for necklaces and brooches. Large stones were the perfect complement to the simplicity of her outfits. She loved mixing imitation and real gems. To keep things interesting, Coco would wear lots of jewelry during the day and avoid all jewelry for an evening look. Her jewelry line became so popular that wealthy ladies with precious gems were now eager to be seen in Chanel imitations.

By 1924, Coco was employing around 3,000 workers. Her perfume was selling reasonably well, but she wanted more Chanel No. 5 sales in all of her stores. Paris' largest department store, Galeries Lafayette, refused to sell it until Coco could provide a larger quantity. The owner, Théophile Bader, suggested she work with Pierre and Paul Wertheimer, owners of France's largest perfume factory.

The first meeting with the Wertheimers left Coco unimpressed. They talked balance sheets and profits while all she wanted was to sell more perfumes. The nitty-gritty details of business bored her. The Wertheimer brothers formed a company especially for Chanel No. 5 named Parfums Chanel. Indifferent, Coco told them to do as they please. All she wanted was ten percent of the French business.

It is likely that Coco didn't understand what she was signing away. The Wertheimers were selling the Chanel brand, but mass merchandizing with advertising campaigns was not Coco's world. Twentieth-century merchandising techniques made for great sales, but now Coco was only receiving ten percent of those profits. She always remained unhappy with this partnership.

By the 1920s, French society was undergoing more changes. The New Woman was coming into her own, wearing her hair short, donning slacks, smoking cigarettes, and experiencing sexual freedom. Women such as Josephine Baker and Colette were engaging in bisexual relationships. In truth, their so-called liberation was more visual than actual. Except for those women entering the workforce, little actually changed in the decade of the flapper.

Coco, who was truly liberated, didn't see herself in competition with men. She adored femininity without the slightest desire to look like a man, stating, "Women who look like men and men who want to look like women are both failures" Although Coco loved fashion, she considered modern dress a mere illusion of freedom. Freedom, she knew, was an attitude, not the correct dress. Her dresses were meant to celebrate the feminine ideal.

During this time, Coco began to design what was to become her most famous garment—the little black dress, which has since become legendary. It was during an evening at the theater that she noticed all the gaudy colors around her. She was appalled. She turned to her companion. "These colors are impossible. These women, I'm bloody well going to dress them in black. I impose black!"

Subsequently, she designed a number of black dresses, both for day and evening. These dresses could be individually accessorized with jewelry, belts, or scarves to create a distinctive look. Coco firmly believed that black drew attention to the individual as well as the dress. *Vogue* agreed in an editorial, stating that Coco's little black dresses were like Ford's black automobiles. It allowed every woman to wear them. The playing field between working women and society women would be leveled.

The 1920s were redefining class membership. Before the war, a working woman such as Coco would never have been accepted in society. Now, Coco herself was employing hordes of Russian aristocrats who could find no other employment. Many of these émigrés had never worked a day in their lives. Coco provided them with dignified work, a fact which quite amused her.

Having grown up in poverty, Coco did care about people. She took in the occasional Russian émigré who was unable to support herself. Believing absolutely that fashion was an important personal statement, she also gave away a dress or two to respectable young women finding themselves in reduced circumstances. If possible, she also hired these women as mannequins in her stores.

Chapter Seven

The Duke of Westminster

"The English are the best people at marrying their mistresses."

—Coco Chanel

Coco lived a lavish lifestyle and could afford generosity. She was regularly interviewed and photographed. Society women wearing Chanel had their dresses noted in the society pages. Coco was about to soar into an entirely different social strata.

Vera Bate, a British socialite, was socially well-placed but short of money following her divorce. Due to her invaluable connections, she was employed at the House of Chanel in the early 1920s. One of Vera's great friends was the duke of Westminster, also known as "Bendor," who happened to be the wealthiest man in England. He was one of the few British aristocrats who had not been forced into reduced circumstances following World War I.

Coco had invited Vera to spend the holidays in Monte Carlo. The duke had his yacht moored nearby and begged Vera for an introduction to the famous Coco Chanel. Coco was hesitant, but Vera persuaded her, insisting they both go. Coco relented, and she accepted the invitation to dine with the duke aboard his yacht. Dinner went well and continued into the casino, where the duke placed large bets. To him, losing money was no big deal.

The duke pursued Coco ardently all the way to Paris. Her suite at the Hôtel de Lauzan was soon filled with exotic flowers and fruit baskets. The duke spared no expenses in his attempt to woo her. When he arrived in Paris, accompanied by the prince of Wales, he personally delivered a bouquet of flowers. His persistence paid off. Coco was ready to be seduced in a grand manner.

Following the war, most of the British aristocracy had been forced to give up their grand lifestyle, servants, and costly mansions. Even the rich among them could no longer afford such homes. That was not the case with the duke of Westminster. His home, Eaton Hall, was maintained by ten housemaids and more than three dozen gardeners. Butlers and housekeepers had their own staff. There were other country estates, including Reay Forest in Scotland, consisting of eight hundred square miles of the best salmon fishing and deer hunting in the country. Winston Churchill was a frequent member of these hunting parties. About Coco, he wrote, "The famous Coco turned up and I took a great fancy to her . . . much the strongest personality Benny [the duke] has been up against."

Their relationship lasted for several years. Coco traveled with the duke to his various estates. She became a skilled fisher and even redecorated his Scottish lodge, Rosehall, in typical Chanel simplicity. She very much adapted herself to the duke's life, something she had not done with her previous lovers. Always the businesswoman, Coco used her visits to Scotland as an inspiration for her tweed collection. These became extremely popular, especially among the British upper classes.

The duke lavished her with stupendous jewels and other gifts. She became quite well-known in royal circles, and when Coco opened a Chanel store in London, the duchess of York and other royal women became immediate customers. Her new tweed outfits were perfect for British country living. Once again, Coco's natural instincts about fashion hit the mark.

The duke was probably the first lover Coco had had who was considering marriage following his second divorce. And she certainly began to consider marriage herself. Coco was vibrant, kept him amused, and would put up with his mistresses. Most importantly, however, the duke wanted more children. Coco, now 44 years old, did everything she could to become pregnant.

In 1927, Coco acquired a piece of land on the French Riviera in order to build a house that would be their home. She hired Robert Streitz to design and build the house, which she would call La Pausa. She took the train from Paris once a month to check on the house's progress. She was extremely exacting, down to the color and shape of the 20,000 roof tiles. Even before she installed lavish furnishings, the cost of the house topped 6 million francs.

While this romantic getaway was being built, her relationship with the Duke became strained. He wanted children, and she wasn't becoming pregnant. In addition, her work on La Pausa left her less time for her business. While her lover drifted to other women, Coco had to endure the public humiliation of her inability to become pregnant and losing another lover. In 1930, the duke of

Westminster married someone else. In a jealous pique, his new wife described Coco as "small, dark and simian."

Still, Coco and the duke remained friends even after their romance was over. A part of Coco was relieved to be able to devote all of her time and energy to her business. La Pausa turned into a lavish home, where she could go and entertain in the style to which she had become accustomed while with the duke of Westminster. Work, however, always took priority.

Chapter Eight

The Crash of 1929

"What rigidity it shows . . . to be frightened by imitations."

—Coco Chanel

The ripple effects of the Wall Street Crash in 1929 were felt throughout Europe. People everywhere had lost up to 90 percent of their assets. Many committed suicide. Coco's clientele was greatly reduced, and she was concerned. The only portion of her business that was still showing a profit was Chanel No. 5, which had become the best-selling perfume in the world. Marilyn Monroe was the first, but certainly not the last, celebrity to endorse Chanel No. 5. Coco herself appeared in several ads.

Not all of the history of Chanel No. 5 is pretty or sexy. Coco had resented her original agreement with the Wertheimer brothers for years, believing she had been swindled. All she ever saw was ten percent of sales from France. The perfume had become a worldwide phenomenon, and she wasn't reaping the benefits.

In the late 1930s, the perfume was being made in Hoboken, New Jersey, using French imports. The Wertheimers were Jewish and at risk of having their business confiscated by the Nazis. Coco's resentment was such that she wrote to a German bureaucrat to regain control of the company. She was surprised to find out that the business-savvy Wertheimers had shifted ownership of the company to a Christian partner. Following World War I, the Wertheimers took back control and arranged for Coco to get two percent of worldwide Chanel No. 5 sales. This made her one of the wealthiest women in the world.

Prior to that, however, Coco found herself in a position to do well despite the crash. Just as Dmitri had been the cause of her meeting with the duke of Westminster, he now introduced Coco to another important personage, Hollywood's Samuel Goldwyn. Goldwyn understood that these difficult times would drive people to escape the reality of joblessness by going to the movies. He intended to make more films than ever. His goal was to draw in more middle-class women, those who would come and gawk at the latest fashion. For that, Goldwyn came to Europe and turned to the number one name in fashion: Coco Chanel.

He wanted Coco to design the dresses worn by his stars, on and off camera. Her dresses would be seen and admired by millions. Goldwyn promised her a million dollars a year if she would come to Hollywood and design outfits for his stars. During these financially precarious times, Coco could use the money. She set sail for America in the spring of 1931.

Goldwyn's orders were that Coco should dress the world's most famous women, such as Greta Garbo, Lillian Gish, and Gloria Swanson, in her fabulous creations. Bets were circulated whether the stubborn couturier could impose her fashion tastes on these equally stubborn stars.

Coco was given a tour of the studio, which did not impress her. She felt the ruthless studio system, especially at MGM, was depriving women of the independence for which she had fought her entire life. She considered actors the servants of the system.

On her way back to Paris to begin her new designs for Hollywood's stars, she stopped in New York to inspect the clothing business there. What she saw amazed her. She was especially fascinated by S. Klein, the enormous discount department store. Klein sold $25 million worth of garments per year. Yet, his store was devoid of any charm or aesthetics. Women had to riffle through the clothes themselves because there were no salespeople to offer assistance to shoppers. Dressing rooms were crowded and public. Clothes were marked down weekly, sometimes to a dollar. These types of discount stores have since become numerous, but at the time, S. Klein was a new experience for Coco, who had worked decades at creating her chic and elegant salons.

Especially following the financial crash, copying couture clothes had become a profitable business. Stores such as S. Klein cheaply reproduced the latest styles in a shoddy manner and with cheap material. For Coco, it was an omen of things to come. Yet unlike other couturiers, Coco remained unworried about her designs being mass-produced. According to her, fashion belonged on the streets, and if it involved copies of her designs, they were still her designs.

Back in Paris, Coco was busy designing dresses for the Goldwyn coterie of stars. The first season went well. Her dresses were spectacular. But the bettors who had their money on the willful stars were ahead of the game. By the second season, stars such as Gloria Swanson refused to wear clothes by the same designer two years in a row. It didn't matter that the designer was the famed Coco Chanel. A part of the problem was the very simplicity for which Coco was known. The last thing the Hollywood elite wanted was simple. Regretfully, Goldwyn was forced to release Coco from her contract.

Still, Goldwyn and Coco remained friends. He used her designs whenever possible. While many famous European designers were facing bankruptcy during these trying times, Goldwyn's two million dollars went a long way to help Coco remain in business. While the stars of Hollywood had rejected her, her association with the movies did enhance her reputation. People who would never enter her salon could now marvel at her creations for the cost of a cinema ticket.

Still, the crash had its effects on the House of Chanel. Her shops were taking in a substantial 120 million francs, but Coco had to make a few changes. Some of her customers were appalled when she substituted cotton for silk to make her clothes more affordable. Many women, however, were happy with her 1933 spring cotton collection. By 1935, her business was back on track. At no time had she lost important customers such as Barbara Hutton and Daisy Fellows. By the end of the year, her staff had increased to 4,000.

Chapter Nine

Chanel during World War II: The Nazi Spy

"Chanel didn't believe in anything, except fashion. Chanel believed in beautiful clothes, she believed in her business and rightly so; she didn't care about Hitler or politics or Nazism."

—Hal Vaughan, author of *Sleeping with the Enemy*

By 1935, a new and bright young designer had burst onto the fashion scene. Elsa Schiaparelli designed skirts and sweaters that were fun and outrageous. Her buttons were shaped like fish; her hats resembled monkeys. The more shocking the color, the better. While more than a decade earlier, Coco has objected to the status quo in fashion and demanded progressive changes, she now found herself protesting the modernity of Schiaparelli.

Coco's dresses hid the waist and bust. Schiaparelli, however, encouraged women to find their curves and display them with pride. Instead of loose, low waists, Schiaparelli jackets were belted tightly to reveal the curves beneath. In the twenties, daring women had worn Chanel; now, in the thirties, the adventuresome lady reached for Schiaparelli. Fashion magazines made much of the rivalry between the two women. Soon enough, Wallis Simpson, the prince of Wales' lover, was photographed wearing Schiaparelli. According to *Vogue,* Coco Chanel was no longer the world's leading clothes designer.

Throughout the 1930s, Coco's daywear retained its simplicity and austerity. Her evening gowns, however, became more dramatic as a result of her rivalry with Schiaparelli. For the first time in her career, Coco was becoming defensive.

The German Army had meanwhile invaded France, and Paris was preparing for bomb attacks in 1939. These were tumultuous times, and those that could escape the city did. Coco was forced to close all of her shops except her original store. Most of her staff was let go. Effectively, the House of Chanel was out of business. Coco remained at the Hotel Ritz, where coincidentally, Schiaparelli also had a suite.

By the summer of 1940, even Coco couldn't delay the inevitable: she had to leave her beloved Paris. She hired a driver to take her to the village of Corbères-Abères in the Pyrenees. She had bought her nephew André Palasse a house there, and it seemed like the ideal refuge. Other refugees soon followed.

When Hitler entered Paris and the city surrendered, Coco was inconsolable. Unable to remain in hiding for long, Coco attempted to return to Paris. Many of the roads were blocked, and petrol was difficult to get. When she finally arrived in Paris, she found the swastika flying from most buildings, including the Ritz. Her suite had been taken over by German officers. She was eventually permitted inside the hotel but was allocated only a small room.

Her one open shop at 31 rue Cambon was filled with German soldiers buying Chanel No. 5 for their wives and girlfriends back home. They socialized freely with the French. The Vichy government had by now totally surrendered to the Nazis.

Coco's actions during the German occupation remain somewhat shrouded. She wasn't overly interested in politics, but she may have considered cooperation with the Nazis a matter of survival. Her only concern was fashion, and the Nazis were in power. Whether it was infatuation or pragmatism, she began an affair with a German officer, Baron Hans Günther von Dincklage. Dincklage saw to it that Coco got her suite at the Ritz back and had unlimited access to petrol during wartime rationing. He also arranged for her nephew, André Palasse, to be released from a prisoner of war camp.

Coco was 46 years old at this point, and no doubt the attention of the handsome and suave German baron was a welcome booster to her spirits. Like all of Coco's lovers, Dincklage was well-born and handsome. He was employed as a diplomat and attaché in Paris, a position that would have involved some information gathering. He specialized in surveilling the activities of Jews. Coco meanwhile turned a blind eye to what was happening around her. She frequently entertained German officers in her hotel suite. Her relationship with Dincklage helped her out, and he, no doubt, received information he could relate back to Berlin.

On June 6, 1944, Allied forces stormed the beaches of Normandy. German forces, including Dincklage, made a hasty retreat. Paris was about to be liberated. Collaborators received harsh treatment at the hands of the new French government. Coco herself was arrested by the Resistance but was mysteriously released within two hours without further explanation. It is believed that members of the British royal family interceded on her behalf. She knew the prince of Wales and was still friendly with the powerful duke of Westminster, as well as Winston Churchill.

It is doubtful that Coco was ever a professional spy for the Nazis, but the woman who had climbed her way to the top didn't hesitate to do what she considered necessary to survive—and to thrive. After the war, she left Paris and fled to Switzerland to avoid further questioning.

Chapter Ten

Exile and Return

"I am against fashion that doesn't last."

—Coco Chanel

Following the war and after selling her beloved La Pausa, Coco moved to Switzerland. She had not reopened her businesses, and there was no longer anything for her to do in Paris. Her work had been her life, and now, she had lost that. Being idle didn't suit her. She moved from elegant hotel to elegant hotel without much purpose. Occasionally, she met up with Dincklage to resume their affair and to give him money. She also took trips to Italy with a variety of lovers and always paid.

By 1954, Paris was no longer the center of fashion. The House of Chanel had been closed for 15 years. New York, and its ready-to-wear apparel, was much sought after. Most of the new designers were male. Dior was all the rage. Coco was infuriated at his designs, which featured tight waists and well-defined breasts. It was everything Coco had argued against as a designer. Finally, she was angry enough to return to Paris.

At the age of 70, Coco Chanel was prepared to get back into the fashion industry. Her showroom had been deserted since the war, with leftover material and aging sewing machines abandoned long ago. She reopened one floor of her old salon and hired only a few assistants to prepare for her newest designs. Her 1954 collection was met with lukewarm praise in Paris. The by-invitation-only showing was met with silence. Too much had changed since Coco had been on top of the fashion world. Also, there were still people who remembered her collaboration with Nazi Germany. Coco Chanel's return proved an utter failure in France.

Not so, however, in other countries. Both the American and British press were enthusiastic. *Vogue* remained an ardent supporter. Coco traveled to America for a private dinner with *Vogue* editor Diana Vreeland. A younger generation of Americans, such as Grace Kelly, Lauren Bacall, and Elizabeth Taylor, was eager to be seen in a Chanel suit. A Chanel creation was once again proof of innate elegance. However, once again, times were changing. By the 1960s, clothing took on the form of defiance. Mary Quant ruled with her mini-dresses that were meant to shock. Coco's response was, "I have no right to criticize, because the time isn't mine. Mine is over."

Coco's last years were lonely ones. Her old friends and lovers were dying, and she was troubled by insomnia. In 1971, Coco was 87 years old. She was still working, busy with her spring showing. On January 9, she felt ill. The following day, she died at the Ritz, where she had lived on and off for 30 years. Her funeral, held at the Église de la Madeleine, was attended by her models, all dressed in Chanel suits. The revelation of her war activities quickly put an end to any grand funeral she might have envisioned. Instead, she was given a quiet and dignified burial.

At the time of her death, Coco Chanel was worth more than 15 billion dollars. While her couture line languished for a few years, Chanel No. 5 continued to explode in popularity. The Wertheimers, who had financed Coco's 1954 return, created a huge marketing campaign meant to attract younger women to the legendary brand. The most famous ad featured Marilyn Monroe, stating, "What do I wear in bed? Chanel No. 5, of course."

During the decades that followed, celebrity photographer Richard Avedon photographed Chanel No. 5 ads featuring Candice Bergen, Nichole Kidman, Catherine Deneuve, and others. The underlying theme was one of luxury and timeless elegance. It remains the world's best-selling perfume.

Designer Karl Lagerfeld took control of the House of Chanel in 1983. He knew he was replacing a legend, and he kept the basic Chanel concepts and adapted them to the twenty-first century. He also introduced a line of men's colognes. Much of what Lagerfeld did was to enhance the legend of Coco Chanel. The name Chanel had been revered for close to a century. Lagerfeld turned the business into a modern fashion icon worth billions. To a younger generation, Lagerfeld himself became a legend.

Conclusion

Coco Chanel worked her way up the ladder of success when women didn't dare show signs of ambition. She understood what women wanted and gave it to them. A hundred years after she designed her first dresses and suits, these items can still be worn with ease. She introduced timelessness and elegance into the fashion world. The name Chanel is synonymous with luxury. Throughout the years, her clothes have been supplemented by handbags, shoes, scarves, a variety of perfumes, and make-up. The Chanel brand has turned into a lifestyle which twenty-first-century fashionable women still desire.

Coco's life is a monument to independence. Some of that independence was achieved by refusing to allow anyone to get too close following the death of her lover, Arthur Capel. Not all of her decisions were good, but she permitted herself the independence to be wrong without guilt. Although she never married or had children, men played an important part in her life. She took lovers when it suited her without apologies. But always, her work remained her top priority.

It is perhaps ironic that despite her years of resentment toward the Wertheimer family, they became the owners of the House of Chanel. The family moved the Chanel headquarters to London, a step which Coco herself would have resented. She considered Paris her only real home. Yet it was the Wertheimers who brought Lagerfeld into the House of Chanel, a step that proved extremely successful for everyone involved.

As generation after generation discovers the Chanel brand, Coco Chanel continues to top the fashion industry even after her death. A true legend never really dies—and that would have suited Coco just fine.

Printed in Great Britain
by Amazon

37280881R00030